33 POEMS

Robert Lax

33 POEMS

edited
by Thomas Kellein

A New Directions Book

With special thanks to Emil Antonucci, Robert Butman, Judith P. Emery, Brother Patrick Hart, Marcia and Jack Kelly, Kenneth Lohf, Bernhard Moosbrugger, and Edward Rice.

Acknowledgments are made to *The New Yorker*, in which "The Man With the Big General Notions," "Zoo Sign," and "Circus" first appeared. Other poems included in this volume were first published in *The Commonweal*, *Dryad*, *Hanging Loose*, *Jubilee*, *Locus Solus*, *The Lugano Review*, *The New York Quarterly*, *Pax*, *Retort*, and *Synapse*. Some of the poems in this volume originally were published by Emil Antonucci at *The Hand Press* (1956), *Journeyman Press* (1959, 1962, 1969, 1970), and by *Tarasque Press* (1971). Other material herein originally appeared in a collection edited by Robert Butman at *pendo-verlag* (1983) or has been brought out in other books by *pendo-verlag* (1981 and 1984).

First published by New Directions in 1988 and reissued in 2019 as New Directions Paperbook 1434.

Library of Congress Cataloguing-in-Publication Data
Names: Lax, Robert, author. | Kellein, Thomas, editor.
Title: 33 poems / Robert Lax ; edited by Thomas Kellein.
Description: New York : New Directions Publishing Corporation, [2019] | "A New Directions book." | Includes bibliographical references.
Identifiers: LCCN 2018053935 | ISBN 9780811228367 (alk. paper)
Subjects: LCSH: American poetry—20th century.
Classification: LCC PS3523.A972 A14 2019 | DDC 811/.54—dc23
LC record available at https://lccn.loc.gov/2018053935

New Directions Books are published for James Laughlin by New Directions Publishing Corporation
80 Eighth Avenue, New York 10011

CONTENTS

the head of the commit-
tee said he couldn't use
it

it shot off, he said, in
too many direc-
tions

throw it onto the junk-
heap, he said,

out there where the wild-
flowers grow

33 POEMS

THE MAN WITH THE BIG GENERAL NOTIONS

A FABLE

There was a man who said, "Why eat cake when all you want is bread? Why eat frosting when all you want is cake? Why eat cake and frosting when all you want is bread and candy?" The man was accounted very wise, and he thought it was a true account.

When he went to build a house he said, "Why get brick when all you want is HARDNESS?"

So he got a big rough stone
And on top of the stone he put a bone
And on top of the bone he put a box
And on top of the box he put a bar
And on top of the bar he put a beam
And the pile stood five feet high
And tottered

And then it fell to the ground.

And the man said, "Why should I get cement when all that I need is STICKINESS?"

So on top of the stone he put some snow
And on top of the bone he put some glue
And on top of the box he put some tape
And on top of the bar he put some gum
And on top of the pile he put molasses

And the pile stood six feet high.

And the man said, "Why should I shingle a roof when all that I want is SHELTER?"

So on top of the pile he put a hat
And next to the hat a big umbrella
And next to that a manhole cover
And next to that a greening tree
And next to that a turtle shell

And the roof was ten feet wide.

Orig. 1939. First publ.
in *The New Yorker*,
Oct. 10, 1942

And the man said, "Why should I get a wife when all that I
want is SOMETHING ALIVE?"

So into the house he put a dog
And next to the dog he put a cat
And next to the cat he put a fish
And next to the fish he put a snail
And next to the snail a big baboon

That stood about four feet high.

"And why should I buy a window or bulb when all that I
want is LIGHT?"

So next to the dog he built a fire
And next to the fire he put a glass
And next to the glass he put a jewel
And next to the jewel an electric eel
And next to the eel a forest pool

Which was about twelve feet deep.

And the man said, "Why should I buy a bed when all that I
want is SLEEP?"

So he went to sleep
And the dog went mad
And bit the cat
And the cat ate the fish
And the fish ate the snail
And the tree caught fire
and the molasses ran
And the snow melted
And the hat fell down
And the cover fell in the forest pool
And so did the shell
And so did the gum
And so did the tape
So did the bar
So did the beam
So did the box
So did the bone
So did the glue
So did the stone.

Some man.

Some house.

ZOO SIGN

At your peril
Feed the squirrel.
Nature is a wolf.

Angry dove
From the branches
Plunges.

Grass will pierce the foot.

Grass will pierce
The angry pigeon.

Lake will swallow
The snarling duck.

Better
Leash the setter
Tighter.

Nature is a wolf.

Orig. 1941. Publ.
in *The New Yorker*,
Oct. 28, 1944

wake up jack
it's 1949

CIRCUS

The silver morning shifts her birds
From tree to tree;
Young green fires burn along the branch;
The river moves but each wave holds a place,
Pattern of knives above the juggling tide.

Now in the south, the circus of the sun
Lays out its route, lifts the white tent,
Parades the pachyderm,
And pins the green chameleon to the cloth.
Coffee-mists rise above the gabbling cook-tent;
Aerialists web above the tumblers' ring;

Behold! In flaming silk, the acrobat,
The wire-walking sun.

Orig. 1949. Publ.
in *The New Yorker*,
May 30, 1953

I was set up from eternity,
And of old,
Before the earth was made:

The depths were not as yet
And I was already conceived;
Neither had the fountains of waters
As yet sprung out;

The mountains with their huge bulk
Had not yet been established;
Before the hills
I was brought forth:

He had not yet made the earth,
Nor the rivers,
Nor the poles of the world:
When he prepared the heavens,
I was there.

(Proverbs 8: 22–27)

THE CIRCUS OF THE SUN

Sometimes we go on a search
and do not know what we are looking for,
until we come again to our beginning...

Orig. 1949–51. Publ. by Emil Antonucci
with *Journeyman Books*, New York 1959.
Also *pendo-verlag*, Zürich 1981

morning

In the beginning (in the beginning of time to say
the least) there were the compasses: whirling in
void their feet traced out beginnings and endings,
beginning and end in a single line. Wisdom danced
also in circles for these were her kingdom: the sun
spun, worlds whirled, the seasons came round, and
all things went their rounds: but in the beginning,
beginning and end were in one.

And in the beginning was love. Love made a sphere:
all things grew within it; the sphere then encompassed
beginnings and endings, beginning and end. Love
had a compass whose whirling dance traced out a
sphere of love in the void: in the center thereof
rose a fountain.

Fields were set
for the circus,
stars for shows
before ever
elephant lumbered
or tent rose.

THE MORNING STARS

Have you seen my circus?
Have you known such a thing?

Did you get up in the early morning and see the
        wagons pull into town?
Did you see them occupy the field?
Were you there when it was set up?

Did you see the cook-house set up in dark
        by lantern-light?
Did you see them build the fire and sit around it
        smoking and talking quietly?

As the first rays of dawn came, did you see
Them roll in blankets and go to sleep?
A little sleep until time came to
Unroll the canvas, raise the tent,
Draw and carry water for the men and animals;
Were you there when the animals came forth,
The great lumbering elephants to drag the poles
And unroll the canvas?

Were you there when the morning moved over the grasses?
Were you there when the sun looked through dark bars of clouds
At the men who slept by the cook-house fire?
Did you see the cold morning wind nip at their blankets?
Did you see the morning star twinkle in the firmament?
Have you heard the voices of the men's low muttering,
Have you heard their laughter around the cook-house fire?
When the morning stars threw down their spears,
        and watered heaven ...

Have you looked at spheres of dew on spears of grass?
Have you watched the light of a star through a world of dew?
Have you seen the morning move over the grasses?
And to each leaf the morning is present.

Were you there when we stretched out the line,
When we rolled out the sky,
When we set up the firmament?
Were you there when the morning stars
        Sang together
And all the sons of God shouted for joy?

12

Morning is quiet over the field. Clouds hang over it close
and full. The song of the morning goes up from the grass;
the sun receives and returns it to clouds, bending over the
morning field, full of the song of the grass.

In a green straw Mexican hat, very gentle and shy,
Tina watches the morning. Belmonte's child. Her hair
is brown and shining, straight. She loves to go out into
her province. Air is summer blue, full of life,
eager to carry light and color.

This is the day when the people come walking slowly
to the outskirts of town; when over the field they come to walk
in the grass where the stakes are driven: rust and dew.
They stand in the morning field, watching.

"See him drag that chain. Look how he pulls it!"
At work in loose pajamas, elephants twist their trunks around
the tent poles lifting lightly, their faces and hides áre
finely lined, maps of a land of mountains and rivers: they move
about in the tall grass,
lifting their great scalloped feet.

13

The men are on hand as witnesses;
"Look at the camel."
"Moulting, I guess."
"There must be something wrong with it."
Inwardly she weeps.

The big stuffed mat the leapers land on sits on the field.
The weary lie on it like Romans; or sit on it upright,
pensively on edge,
like little big-headed Bagonghi.
Thinking about his teeth. "I go downtown to see the dentist,
every day, every day."
Every day a different town.

The festivity of plumes on timothy grass,
water-filled young shoots up from the early ground aspiring,
up in the early morning playing, they are wet with water of
sky, sprinkled by clouds, standing,
overshoulder peering at light on the field;
dart of birds, and look here: walkers walking in sky water;
drops on grass, hanging colors: light of sun in many colors,
all the colors, and the drop stands on the timothy grass
wondering will I fall to earth or will I rise to heaven?

Up every day for the festival,
today is the festival of walkers, walking:
Out of all the round year today, the day of its coming.
We the innocent grasses stand on tiptoes overshouldering
each other, looking toward the circle's center,
middle of the field where they stretch the skyworks.
Birds dart over us, pulling shadows through us.

Quietly the field waited;
She would be blessed with the wonder of creation.
Workers are arrived from another world; like visiting angels,
they speak their own language and put their questioners
off with jokes: rough trousers, blue denim shirts, flesh red
from the elements:
Their eyes look far back, and infinitely on. They penetrate
and do not appraise:
beholding all things before them with the innocence of light.
Strange visitors, when they meet
they fall to laughter,
their glances flash together like water in sunlight.

These are the ones who tug at the ropes and put up the tents;
roustabouts with chants and hammers, who drive the stakes that
hold in place the billowing firmament.

Bagonghi says, "I'll take your suitcase until Mogador
wakes up."

Stubby, bow-legged, he rocks from side to side, a tug in a
swell, as he crosses the field,
holding the bag an inch above the ground.
He opens the wide door of the trailer, stands on tip-toes,
swings the suitcase into the dark. "It'll be all right till
Mogador wakes up."
He comes back leaving the door ajar.

The ground of the field is rich and growing, but who
will eat the grass? Horses, camels, zebras.

A song rises up from the ground, herbs from the field. Who will watch the green grass growing; who will hear the song of earth?

Children who come to see the tent set up in the morning.

Three masts stand on a sea of canvas. Rope line loops from one to another, drops in a gentle arc to the ground. Bagonghi swings his hand toward the gesture in mid-air.

"Look! The big top!"

Who stretches forth the canopy of morning?

(Knowing the wonder to be born of her, hoping to bring forth a son, a tree, in whose laughing and delicate shade the children of innocence could rejoice, the field waited.)

We have seen all the days of creation in one day: this is
the day of the waking dawn and all over the field the
people are moving, they are coming to praise the Lord:
and it is now the first day of creation. We were there on
that day and we heard Him say: Let there be light. And
we heard Him say: Let firmament be; and water, and
dry land, herbs, creeping things, cattle and men. We were
there in the beginning for we were there in the morning
and we saw the rising of the tent and we have known how
it was in the beginning. We have known the creation of
the firmament: and of the water, and of the dry land, and
of the creatures that moved in the deep, and of the crea-
tures that moved on the land, and of the creation of men:
the waking of acrobats. We have known these things from
the beginning of the morning, for we woke early. We rose
and came to the field.

They lie in slumber late, the acrobats;
They sleep and do not know the sun is up.

Nor does the Lord wake them,
Nor do the sun's rays touch them.

And the Lord, who has chosen them,
The Lord, who created them,

Leaves them in slumber until it is time.

Slowly, slowly, His hand upon the morning's lyre
Makes a music in their sleeping.

And they turn, and turning wonder
Eyes awake to light of morning.

They rise, dismounting from their beds,

They rise and hear the light airs playing

Songs of praise unto the Lord.

The circus is a song of praise,

A song of praise unto the Lord.

The acrobats, His chosen people,
Rejoice forever in His love.

Mogador comes down the field.

"There he is!"

He walks the earth like a turning ball: knowing
and rejoicing in his sense of balance:
he delights in the fulcrums
and levers, teeter-boards, trampolines, high-wires,
swings, the nets, ropes and ring-curbs of the natural
universe.

Beneath his feet the world is buoyant,
thin and alive as a bounding rope.
He stands on it poised,
a gyroscope on the rim of a glass,
sustained by the whirling of an inner wheel.

He steps through the drum of light and air, his
hand held forth.
The moment is a sphere moving with Mogador.

ACROBAT'S SONG

Who is it for whom we now perform,
Cavorting on wire:
For whom does the boy
Climbing the ladder
Balance and whirl –
For whom,
Seen or unseen
In a shield of light?

Seen or unseen
In a shield of light,
At the tent top
Where rays stream in
Watching the pin-wheel
Turns of the players
Dancing
In light:

Lady,
We are Thy acrobats;
Jugglers;
Tumblers;
Walking on wire,
Dancing on air,
Swinging on the high trapeze:
We are Thy children,
Flying in the air
Of that smile:
Rejoicing in light.

20

Lady,
We perform before Thee,
Walking a joyous discipline,
A thin thread of courage,
A slim high wire of dependence
Over abysses.

What do we know
Of the way of our walking?
Only this step,
This movement,
Gone as we name it.
Here
At the thin
Rim of the world
We turn for Our Lady,
Who holds us lightly:
We leave the wire,
Leave the line,
Vanish
Into light.

The tent is soaked in afternoon light. Filled with sound.
Pilgrims wander in at the wide door, full of wonder.
The expanse of it!

Waving walls.
Tiers of seats.
Can this have been built in one day?

They enter; parents guiding: they have seen more places.
Yet look: a child is leading.

Filled with wonder; the tent is strange;
circus horses and circus men.
Clowns are from a far-off land.

The tent shuts out the wind, and heat, the dust and rain, and locks
light in.

Through the wide door: they roll like marbles; first a few, and
later many.
Tent-flap leads to the field beyond: performers cross;
their plumed hats shake; their red and gold capes
billow in the wind.

The family
Running lightly into the ring,
Lead one horse with them
And leave two others standing in the track.
There is a flourish of trumpets.
The Cristianis approach the center of the ring,
Raise their hands,
Smile,
and bow.
The music starts again;

The horse trots rhythmically around the ring,
Five Cristianis stand in a row,
Marking time,
In rhythm with the hoof-beats.
At a signal from Lucio
They run across the ring
To meet the horse
When he comes around.
They fork-jump as he passes
And land all sitting on his back.

                                    Applause.

The horse runs halfway around;
The riders relaxed
Lift their hands to show how easily it is done.
Then they leap off,
Belmonte first,
Corky,
Ortans,
Mogador
And Oscar.
Once more raise their hands and smile.

Music again,
The horse starts around
And the boys,
Belmonte,
Mogador,
Oscar

Make jumps to his back,
Land standing with arms upraised.
Leaping separately
But riding together.

As they come around
Lucio,
In baggy pants,
Oversized jacket and battered hat,
Steps out in front of the horse.

The boys shout: "Hey! get out of the way!"
Lucio doesn't.
The boys jump down from the horse.
"Get out of the way. What are you? Drunk?"

Lucio shrugs,
Walks over to the ring
Sits down, begins to ponder.

Again music.

The boys begin their run to the horse
When Lucio slides across the ring
Somersaults through the horse's legs
Over the ring curb
Onto the track.

                                                    Gasp.

He tries again from outside the ring.
Somersaults through the flying hooves
Into the ring.

Picking up a bamboo pole
He vaults magnificently
To the horse's back.
Trembling he lands
Standing on one foot
Flailing his arms,
Sure to topple.

Shouts.

At last he finds it:
The point of balance
Secure,
Both feet planted firmly,
He leans back
Thumbs in his pockets:
Never a doubt in his mind.

He pulls a newspaper from his hip pocket,
Slaps it open, begins to read,
Then turning
Still reading
He takes a huge step
Off the horse's tail
Like an old man
Descending from a bus.

PENELOPE AND MOGADOR

One time Penelope the tightrope-walker asked Mogador
how he was able to land so gracefully after he did a
somersault on horse-back.
Mogador said:

> It is like a wind that surrounds me
> Or a dark cloud,
> And I am in it,
> And it belongs to me
> and it gives me the power
> to do these things.

And Penelope said, Oh, so that is it.
And Mogador said, I believe so.
The next day in the ring, Mogador leaped up on the horse.
He sat on it sideways and jogged half-way around the ring;
Then he stood up on the horse's back with a single leap;
He rode around balancing lightly in time to the music;
He did a split-jump – touching his toes with his hands;
He did a couple of entrechats – braiding his legs in
mid-air like a dancer:
Then Oscar threw him a hoop.
Mogador tossed it up in the air and spun it.
He caught it,
Leapt up,
And did a somersault through it!
He thought:

> I am a flame,
> A dark cloud,
> A bird;
> I will land like spring rain
> on a mountain lake
> For the delight of Penelope
> the tightrope-walker;

He landed on one foot, lost his balance, waved his arms
wildly, and fell off the horse.

He looked at Penelope,
Leapt up again,
Did a quick entrechat,
And Oscar tossed him the hoop.
He spun it into the air and caught it.

He did a somersault through it
And he thought:
> It is like a dark cloud, and I am in it;
> It belongs to me,
> And it gives me the power
> To do these things.
He landed on one foot, lost his balance, waved his arms
wildly and fell off the horse.
Penelope the tightrope-walker looked very calm.
Mogador leapt on the horse again.
Oscar frowned and tossed him the hoop.
He threw it into the air and caught it;
Leapt up and did a somersault through it.
He thought:
> I am a bird and will land like a bird!
He landed on one foot, lost his balance, waved his arms wildly
and fell off the horse.
> Now in the Cristiani family, when you fall off three times,
> They grab you by one ear,
> And bend you over,
> And one of the brothers
> Kicks you.
And that is what they did to Mogador.
Then the circus band started playing again.
And Mogador looked at Penelope:
Then he looked at the horse and flicked his ear with his hand;
He jumped up on the horse and landed smartly;
He stood up in one leap and caught the hoop;
He twirled it in the air and caught it again;
And then he did a somersault through it.
He didn't think anything.
He just did a somersault –
And landed with two feet on the horse's back.
Then he rode half-way around the ring
And got off with a beautiful scissors leap.
Penelope applauded,
And clasping her hands overhead, shook them
> like a boxer.
Mogador looked at her,
> then back at the horse,
And with a gesture of two arms he said
It was nothing.

ORTANS

Ortans stands on one end of a teeter-board:
Mogador and Belmonte,
From the height of two tables
Jump
Down
And
Land
On the other end.

Ortans flips into the air,
Does a two and a half turn
And lands neatly in a high chair.
Relaxed as a rag doll,
Gracious as a queen,
Looking as though she had been there all afternoon.
She lolls a moment in the chair,
Gives the audience a glance
And a beautiful smile.

Then she daintily dismounts
Into her brothers' arms;
Lifts her right hand,
Curtseys on tiptoes and disappears.

LA LOUISA

Her toes almost touch the top of the tent;
She lies out, balanced at the arch of her back,
Her toes are pointed,
Her long slim legs stretch before her,
Her waist is taut,
Her whole body is semi-relaxed.

Her arms lie out gracefully behind her head,
Her long hair rides behind her as she swings forward:
There is a flower in her hair,
It hugs her head as she swings back.

Back and forth,
Back and forth.

Now she drops.
Head first:
Her hair
And the flower
Tumbling toward the ground.
Look away!

Precipito-
volissimo-
volmente!

She has caught herself,
Is hanging by her feet;
She swings back and forth,
Her back beautifully arched,
Her hands and fingers poised,
The flower riding in her long hair.

She pulls herself up,
Hangs by her hands,
Grasps the rope between her legs,
Slides down it to the ground.

Bows graciously,
Accepts applause
with lifted arm,

And leaves the ring.

Our dreams have tamed the lions,
have made pathways in the jungle,
peaceful lakes; they have built new
Edens ever-sweet and ever-changing
By day from town to town we carry
Eden in our tents and bring its won-
ders to the children who have lost
their dream of home.

evening

They are with me now, the golden people; their limbs
are intertwined in golden light, moving in a heavy sea
of memory: they come, the beautiful ones, with evening
smiles: heavy-lidded people, dark of hair and gentle
of aspect, whose eyes are portals to a land of dusk.
Their melancholy holds me now: sadness of princes, and
the sons of princes: the melancholy gaze of those I
have not seen since childhood.

For childhood was full of wonder, full of visions: the
boy on horseback, either in a dream or on the plain,
approaching: the two gypsy girls who stood together and
asked the mysterious question. Truth and the dream so
mingled in their eyes I could not tell which of the two
had spoken.

Once more now they are with me, golden ones,
living their dream in long afternoons of sunlight;
riding their caravans in the wakeful nights.

After supper light on fields, prairie, long yellow
light on fields aspiring, fields looking up grass singing
high grass singing yellow light on green grass growing,
the wide round horizon, the long tired light on the field
and the green grass high yearning up aspiring to heaven
to the dome sky heaven the grass growing up to the sky
and the light dying, the sun wearily sleepily smiling
lying down, with a sighing song, a long smiling sigh
over the fields and the grass rising, thin prayer rising
tufted to the air above the field to the sky the dome
sky thin made of light air the dome above the field and
the field breathing the air full rich golden grass smelling
sweet and tired with sun dying sun lying down, dying down
in west.

The sunset city trembled with fire, the air trembled
in fiery light, a fiery clarity stretched west across the
walks, the tongues of air licked up the building sides, the
wings of fire hovered over the churches and houses, steeples
and stores of the wide flat city that stretched to the sea.
The walk like a drum was stretched as though over the
hollow kettle of ground, the hollow darkness under the walk
resounded as he walked toward the sunset, and the street
glowed like a drum in firelight, like a drumskin glowed the
walk and road as he walked toward the light, walked slowly
toward the light through the fiery clarity of the burning
air now cooled with evening as sun set. Walls of glass
reflected the fire of sun, took fire from it, were kindled
and blazed bright, so as he walked down the drumskin city,
he was walled in fire and walked toward fire, and in the
fire dark caverns were, dark door-ways in the walls of fire,
portals in the panes of brass where these men sat on folding
camp chairs waiting while the world went round, bald men
sat on folding camp chairs waiting while the world went
round, their drumskin heads took fire from the sun, kindled
and blazed, were copper drums, brass helmets glowing above
the drumskin walks, each in his dark portal surrounded,
tipped on his campstool in door's darkness; brass accent
in the walls of glass. In the fiery city they sat on
campstools waiting while the world went round.

This is our camp, our moving city; each day we
set the show up: jugglers calm amid currents, riding
the world, joggled but slightly as in a howdah, on
the grey wrinkled earth we ride as on elephant's
head.

THE DUST OF THE EARTH

The dust of the day hangs in the air,
Motes in the light,
Dust of the trampling multitude,
Dust of the elephants padding by,
Dust no one stirred till the circus came,
It hangs like a veil!
Dust of the earth
Riding the twilight,
Silently moving
Each sphere
Each molecule
Riding the air,
In wakening twilight
Could
Whirling
Turn to earth
To planets,
Support the verdure of creation
The moving animals and men,
Could raise from its own green growing
White clouds and dark
Alive with lightning,
Could ripple with seas
Flow with rivers
Reflect the waters,
The mountains and sky.

But where does the first mote come from,
The first gliding sphere?

the midway

The paintings on the sideshow walls,
The banners and signs
Are dark and strange:
"Look at the two-headed boy, the armless wonder,
The lion-tamer,
The harlem band,
The seal boy,
The sword swallower,
Fire-eater,
Tattooed woman,
Snake charmer
And the man who throws knives at his wife."

In the darkening twilight,
The last of sunset.
Banners
Heraldic and strange:
Beowulf lives here,
Ogres inside,
But gay, strange music,
Come in and look,
Stand considering on the midway
Soon you will come in and look.

SNAKE CHARMER

"You see this snake?
He looks terrible, don't he?
But in the southwest where I come from
We got 'em like cats to kill mice."
She strokes his head,
Folds him gently,
And puts him back in the box.

Picking out a larger one,
She holds it aloft in both arms:
"This here is the same kind of snake,"
She says,
"Only bigger."

DOG ACT

Girl in white ten-gallon hat, jewelled band;
white shirt jewelled sleeves;
white gauntlets jewelled with flowers and stars;
skirt, white doe-skin, fringed;
spurred and jewelled high-heeled boots,
white with red interior,
striding in a wash of small white dogs.

Yapping, prancing, barrel-walking,
ladder-climbing, table-mounting,
somersaulting
hopping at her hissed command
through tiny shiny hoops.

COLONEL ANGUS

"I don't remember where he lived out there," said the
Colonel.
"I think it was ... aaaah! that lion!"

It was time for him to go on;
The lion knew it and roared.

The Colonel went into the small cage carrying a folding
chair and a whip.
The lion, big and dusty snarled and pawed at him,

Then he roared,
Angus snapped the whip,
The lion crouched and pounced.
Apparently alarmed,
The trainer dropped his chair,
Scurried from the cage,
Slipped through the steel door and sprung it behind him.
The audience was impressed.
The lion, furious, was left standing with his paws against
the door.

"I think it was Pasadena!" said the Colonel coming lightly
down the steps.

night

ACROBAT ABOUT TO ENTER

Star of the bareback riding act,
Dressed in a dark-red high-collared cape,
Black-browed,
Waiting with the others
To go in:

To enter
The bright yellow
Glare of the tent,

He stood on an island,
Self-absorbed.

At twenty-one
There was trouble in his universe.

Stars were falling;
Planets made their rounds
With grating axles:

The crown of stars in blackness
Was awry.

Clouds were rising,
Thunder rumbled;
He was alone,
Nobly troubled
Waiting a moment.

He waited with challenge,
Young and in solitude,
Mourning inwardly,
Attentive to the black, fiery current
In his mind,
He would not be comforted.

Swift water,
Falling darkness:
He alone could hear it.

Hoarded the sound,
Pulled his cape around it:
Bitter and intense,
But it was his:

Youthful secret,
Black and smouldering,
Not of the crowd;

It was his private woe,
And being private,
Prized.

Now in telling the story
Of the Cristianis
Their early beginning
And long-ago birth
And their rising from earth
To brightness of sunlight,
We tell of creation
And glory,
Of rising,
And fall:
And again of the rising
Where we are all risen;
For each man redeemed
Is risen again.

The spinning of the sun,
The spinning of the world,
The spun sun's span
On the world in its spinning,
Are all in the story
From its beginning;
And when it is spun
There shall be no unspinning.

Mogador is running along with the horse.
His eyes are serious, full of thought.
His mouth is a little open as he runs and breathes.
He is smiling a little.
His lips are thin.

As he runs,
Bending the knees,
Dancing lightly beside the horse,
He is in step with the horse.

They both land lightly.
They spring both from the earth;
Their movement is through the air.
Their feet drop lightly to earth
And push off from it.

And as they rise and fall,
Rise,
Fly,
And (momentarily) fall,
Their heads rise too
And fall in regular rhythm.

They rise
And the hair of the horse's mane clings to him,
Pointing to earth.

They drop down
And each hair of the white long mane
Remains in air

The boy's hair too,
Dark silk
Rides close as he rises;
Then rises in the air
Falling lightly over his forehead
As he drops to earth.

They come around the ring.
The boy runs on the inside.
The horse trots along close to the curb.

The boy with his horse as they turn
in the ring are boy and horse running in
blue and green field: his hand is on the
horse's back the horse is to him close as hand.

They round the turn, the boy is out of sight.
But now, behold!
He flies above the horse, holding a strap at his shoulders.
His feet fly out behind.
His toes are together and pointed like closed scissors.
Now he splits,
Sits riding bareback
Pointing his toes to the ground
Spinning beneath them.
His arms are held in air relaxed.

He rides lightly,
Barely touching,
His arms in air.
Then he leaps up
And with a pirouette begins his dance.
What was begun
As a run
through the field
is turned
to ritual.

RASTELLI

Now the story of Rastelli is one they love to tell
Around the circus
He is a hero
Not because his work was dangerous
But because he was excellent at it
And because he was excellent as a friend.

He was good at juggling
At talking
At coffee

Loving everyone
He died juggling
For everyone

He died
Oscar said in a low secret voice
when he was 33

The age of our Lord

They loved Rastelli
And he loved them
Their loves flamed together
A high blaze

Ascending to the Sun of being

Rastelli was a juggler and a kind of sun
His clubs and flames and hoops
Moved around him like planets
Obeyed and waited his command
He moved all things according to their natures:
They were ready when he found them
But he moved them according to their love.

As dancers harmonize, the rising falling planets
mirrored his movements.
Rising, falling, rotating, revolving they spun on
the axis of his desire.

Clubs were at rest, he woke them and sent them spinning;
From which again they flew, until flying and falling,
Spinning and standing a moment in midair,
They seemed to love to obey his command,
And even dance with the juggler.

Seeing the world was willing to dance,
Rastelli fell in love with creation,
Through the creation with the Creator,
And through the Creator again with creation
And through the creation, the Lord.

He loved the world and things he juggled,
He loved the people he juggled for.
Clubs and hoops could answer his love:
Even more could people.

Lover and juggler
Bearer of light
He lived and died in the center ring
Dancing decorously
Moving all things according to their nature

And there, before the Lord, he dances still.

He is with us on the double somersault;
The three-high to the shoulders;
He is with us on the Arab pirouette and the principal
act on horseback.
And in the long nights,
Riding the trucks between towns, Rastelli is with us:
Companion,
Example,
Hero in the night of memory.

He stood outside the horse truck, waiting for Mogador to
come back and he began to whistle. Across the field the men
had taken down the sides of the tent and were moving about in
dim light under the top, picking up trunks, ropes and equipment
and packing it away. He began to whistle a tune from the
depths of his soul; he had never heard it before but he
recognized it as a form of the song his soul had always been
singing, a song he had been singing since the beginning of
the world, a song of return. It was as though he stood in a
dark corner of the universe and whistled softly, between his
teeth, and the far stars were attentive, as though he whistled
and waves far off could hear him, as though he had discovered
a strain at least of the night song of the world.

By day I have circled like the sun,
I have leapt like fire.

At night I am a wise-man
In his palanquin.

By day I am a juggler's torch
Whirling brightly.

Have you known such a thing?
That men and animals
Light and air,
Graceful acrobats,
And musicians
Could come together
In a single place,
Occupy a field by night
Set up their tents
In the early morning
Perform their wonders
In the afternoon
Wheel in the light
Of their lamps at night?

Have you seen the circus steal away?
Leaving the field of wonders darkened,
Leaving the air, where the tent stood, empty,
Silence and darkness where sight and sound were,
Living only in memory?

Have you seen the noon-day banners
Of this wedding?

THE JUGGLER

The juggler
is throwing
and catching,
standing
where the tent
flaps open,
practicing
his art.

Hours a day
with indian clubs,
steadily moving;
if one of them drops,
he moves very slowly,
bending
and reaching
to pick it up.

Two from the right hand,
two from the left,
and catching two and two;
one from the right,
and one from the left,
one from the right,
and one from the left;
catching them
one by one.

They wing
through the air,
they fly like birds;
they land

Orig. 1952. Publ. by Emil
Antonucci with *The Hand Press*,
New York 1956

in his hand
like pigeons
roosting;
they are clubs turning,
whirling,
birds flying,
comets falling;
they are
fields
moving,
fields of light
moving,
circling,
flying,
being moved
from hand to hand.

His hand
sends flying,
his hand
brings home;
but there is a law
in earth and air
to make
the bird
return.

Between his turns
the juggler stands
holding his clubs,
resting his weight,
watching the earth.

Again he is swift,
is agile,
full of wit;
he commands
and they follow;
he sends them spinning
where they intend to go.

He is here,
is there,
moving swiftly:
one who hides
from cloud
to spring
to mountain-cleft,
to a voice
within a flame.

He leans back
and throws them
over his head,
two at a time,
two at a time,
catching
and throwing:

Under his right leg,
under his left,
under his right leg,
under his left;
his solemn dancing
is only a way
of letting the clubs
go by.

The juggler
is playing,
throwing and catching,
resting,
returning;
practicing
his art.

JERUSALEM

reading of lovely Jerusalem,
lovely, ruined Jerusalem.

we are brought to the port
where the boats in line are
and the high tower on he hill
and the prows starting again
into the mist.

for we must seek
by going down,
down into the city
for our song.
deep into the city
for our peace.
for it is there
that peace lies
folded
like a pool.

there we shall seek:
it is from there
she'll flower.

for lovely, ruined Jerusalem,
lovely, sad Jerusalem
lies furled
under the cities
of light.

for we are only
going down,
only descending
by this song
to where the cities
gleam in darkness,

Orig. 1954. Publ.
in *Jubilee*, Feb. 1956

or curled like roots
sit waiting
at the undiscovered
pool.

what pressure
thrusts us up
as we descend?

pressure of
the city's singing,

pressure of
the song
she hath withheld.

hath long withheld.

for none
would hear
her.

QUESTION

If you were an alley violinist

And they threw you money
from three windows

And the first note contained
a nickel and said:

"When you play, we dance and
sing" signed
A very poor family

And the second one contained
a dime and said:

"I like your playing
very much!" signed
A sick old lady

And the last one contained
a dollar and said:
"Beat it"

Would you

1. Stand there and play?
2. Beat it?
3. Walk away playing your fiddle?

Orig. ca. 1958. First publ.
in *PAX* # 14, 1961

the port
was longing

the port
was longing

not for
this ship

not for
that ship

not for
this ship

not for
that ship

the port
was longing

the port
was longing

not for
this sea

not for
that sea

not for
this sea

not for
that sea

the port
was longing

the port
was longing

Orig. 1960. First publ.
in *Locus Solus* # III–IV,
Winter 1962

not for
this &

not for
that

not for
this &

not for
that

the port
was longing

the port
was longing

not for
this &

not for
that.

one stone
one stone
one stone

i lift
one stone
one stone

i lift
one stone
and i am
thinking

i am
thinking
as i lift
one stone

one stone
one stone
one stone

i lift
one stone
one stone

i lift
one stone
and i am
thinking

i am
thinking
as i lift
one stone

i am
thinking
as i lift
one stone
one stone

Orig. 1960. First publ. in
"R. L.: New Poems", ed. Emil
Antonucci with *Journeyman
Books*, New York 1962

i am
thinking
as i lift
one stone

one stone
one stone
one stone

i lift
one stone
one stone

i lift
one stone
and i am
thinking

i am
thinking
as i lift
one stone:

one stone
one stone
one stone

one stone
one stone
one stone

one stone
one stone

one stone
one stone

one stone
one stone
one stone

ANDALUSIAN PROVERB

rooster
rooster
rooster

rooster
with your
head cut
off:

what
are you
thinking
now,

you rooster,
what are you
thinking now
of the bloody
morning?

Orig. 1960.
First publ. ibid.

The Maximum Capacity
of this room
is 262 people

262 people

The Maximum Capacity
of this room
is 262 people

Orig. 1960.
First publ. ibid.

forms
forms
forms

basic
basic
forms

basic
basic
basic
basic
basic
basic
forms

Orig. 1960
First publ. ibid.

the first goodbye
the second goodbye
the third goodbye
the fourth goodbye
the fifth goodbye
the sixth goodbye
the seventh goodbye
the eighth goodbye
the ninth goodbye
the tenth goodbye
the eleventh goodbye
the twelfth goodbye
the hundred & twenty-first goodbye
the hundred & forty-fourth goodbye
the hundred & eighty-ninth goodbye
goodbye
goodbye
goodbye

Orig. 1960.
First publ. ibid.

one bird
two birds

one bird
two birds

two birds
one bird

two birds
one bird

one bird
two birds

one bird
two birds

two birds
one bird

two birds
one bird

one

Orig. 1960.
First publ. ibid.

river
river
river

river
river
river

river
river
river

river
river
river

Orig. 1961.
Publ. in *Synapse*
2, 1964

in the dark
in the dark
my love
is lying
in the
park

my love
is lying
in the park
and listening
to the stream

. . . .
. . . .
. . . .
. . . .

in the dark
in the dark
my love
is lying
in the park

my love
is lying
in the park
and listening
to the stream

Orig. 1961. First publ. in "R. L.: New Poems",
ed. Emil Antonucci with *Journeyman Books*,
New York 1962

SHORTER
HISTORY
OF WESTERN
CIVILIZATION

Egyptians
Babylonians
Persians

Egyptians
Babylonians
Persians

Jews &
Greeks

Jews &
Greeks

Egyptians
Babylonians
Persians

Egyptians
Babylonians
Persians

Jews &
Greeks

Jews &
Greeks

Orig. 1961. Publ. in *The Commonweal*
Vol. LXXXV, # 21, Feb. 16, 1962

Christians
Christians
Christians

Christians
Christians
Christians

Christians
Christians
Christians

rah
rah
rah

"are you a visitor?" asked
the dog.

"yes," i answered.

"only a visitor?" asked
the dog.

"yes," i answered.

"take me with you," said
the dog.

Orig. 1961. First publ. in "R. L.: New Poems",
ed. Emil Antonucci with *Journeyman Books*,
New York 1962

in me
in me
in me

is the
watcher

in me
in me
in me

is the
watcher

in me
is the
watcher

in me
is the
watcher

in me
in me
in me

is the
watcher

Orig. 1961.
First publ. ibid.

every
night
in the
world

is a
night

in the
hospital

Orig. 1961.
First publ. ibid.

THE BOMB

SCENARIO FOR AUDITORIUM

Orig. ca. 1961.
Unpublished

SCENE: a public square. Big city. In center: a fountain.
Crowds milling, talking

VOICES:

jabba
jabba
jabba
jabba

wook
wook
wook
wook

jabba
jabba
jabba
jabba

wook
wook
wook
wook

jabba
jabba
jabba

wook
wook

w . . .

[interrupted.]

SOUND:

siren
[alarm]
silence
[12 seconds-
24 seconds]

VOICES:

[resume]

jabba
jabba
jabba
jabba

wook
wook
wook
wook

jabba
jabba
jabba
jabba

wook
wook
wook
wook

jab . . .

SOUND:

siren
[silence
again.
32 seconds]

VOICES:

[slowly
resumes:]

jab
jabba
jabba

jabba
jabba
jabba
jabba

wook
wook
wook
wook

jabba
jabba
jabba
jabba

wook
wook
wook
wook

[louder]

wook
wook
wook
wook

jabba
jabba
jabba
jabba

wook
wook
wook
wook

jabba
jabba
jabba
jabba

wook
wook
wook

SOUND:

B W O O M !
[The Bomb.]

Square is blasted with white (and at same time many-colored) light.
Deafening, splitting, screaming sound which holds for 3–4–5–6 seconds.
Then blackness.

Then resumption of grey light on ruins. Twisted fountain, broken down.

SPOTLIGHTS: one strong, pink; one blue, shoot one by one through dim
daylight to pick out figures: man draped across fountain; woman supine
across bench or rock. Human figures like dummies, piled. Horror masks.
One man, still alive, staggers, stalks across stage blasted [left to
right], howling wildly. Is he holding a child?

SEA & SKY

Orig. 1963. Publ. in *The Lugano Review*
Vol. I, # 3–4, September 1965

I.

they
groan

why
do
they
groan

the
people
groan

why
do
the
people
groan

the
nations
groan

why
do
the
nations
groan

?

why
do
the
nations
groan

&
why
do
they
re-
peat

a
vain
thing

?

the
clouds

the
clouds

are
ris-
ing

(over
the
sea)

the
winter

the
winter

(is
com-
ing)

sit
closer

to-
geth-
er

sit
closer

as
well

to
the
earth

(for
the
cold

comes
on)

the
earth

the
earth

in
all
its
seasons

in
all
its
seasons

in
all
its
seasons

the
earth

the
earth

the
earth

not

thus

&
thus

&
thus

&
thus

but

thus

&
thus

&
thus

not

thus

&
thus

&
thus

&
thus

but

thus

&-
thus

&
thus

a
cer-
tain
rhythm

a
cer-
tain
know-
ing

to
be
ob-
serv-
'd

to
be
re-
mark-
'd

a
cer-
tain
rhythm

a
cer-
tain
know-
ing

(in
all

the
chang-
ing

days)

praris-
ing

this
mo-
ment

with
all

of
his
heart

gave
him
heart

gave
him
heart

for
the
next

prais-
ing

this

mo-
ment

with
all

of
his
heart

gave
him
heart

gave
him
heart

for
what
fol-
low
'd

prais-
ing

this
mo-
ment

with
all

of
his
heart

gave
him
heart

gave
him
heart

for
what
fol-
low-
'd

prais-
ing

this
mo-
ment

with
all

of
his
heart

gave
him
heart

gave
him
heart

for
what
fol
low-
'd

the
light

the
light

the
eye

the
eye

the
eye

the
eye

the
light

the
light

the
light

the
light

the
eye

the
eye

the
eye

the
eye

the
light

the
light

the
sun

the
sun

the
city

the
city

the
city

the
city

the
sun

the
sun

no
more

the
sun

no
more

the
sun

the
city

the
city

no
more

no
more

no
more

the
sun

no
more

the
sun

the
city

the
city

(no
more)

the
city

the
city

the
city

the
city

the
sun

the
sun

the
sun

the
city

the
city

the
city

the
city

(the
city

the
city)

the
sun

the
city

the
city

(a
sun-
less
cit-
y)

the
city

the
city

(the
sun)

the
city

the
city

(a
sun-
less
cit-
y)

the
city

the
city

(the
sun)

why
do
the
na-
tions

groan

why
do
the
na-
tions

trem-
ble

why
do
the
na-
tions

groan

&
trem-
ble

(&
the
peo-
ple

re-
peat

a
vain

thing)

?

II.

the
world

the
world

with-
in

with-
in

the
world

the
world

with-
in

with-
in

the
world

the
world

with-
in

with-
in

that
sings

that
sings

that
sings

salt
salt

sweet
salt

no
tear

of
cloud

no
tear

con-
tains

sea's
wis-
dom

salt

sweet

salt

salt
salt

sweet
salt

no
tear

of
cloud

no
tear

con-
tains

sea's
wis-
dom

salt

sweet

salt

the
fire

the
fire

of
thorn

of
thorn

the
fire

the
fire

of
thorn

of
thorn

of
thorn

of
thorn

a
fire

a
fire

a
fire

a
fire

of
thorn

the
dove

the
dove

the
dove

the
dove

comes
down

comes
down

&
breaks

the
air

the
dove

the
dove

the
dove

the
dove

comes
down

&
breaks

the
air

look
look

what
circles

these

now
whis-
per

whis-
per

through

the
sea

look
look

what
circles

these

now
whis-
per

(end-
less)

through

the
seas

the
words

the
words

of
heav-
'n

re
fin-
'd

re-
fin-
'd

re-
fin-
'd

re-
fin-
'd

the
words

the
words

of
heav-
'n

re-
fin-
'd

the
words

the
words

of
heav-
'n

re-
fin-
'd

all

a-
like

&
all

the
same

all

a-
like

&
all

the
same

no-
thing

no-
thing

no-
thing

chang-
es

no-
thing

no-
thing

no-
thing

new

III.

black
the
warp

&
red
the
woof

black
the
warp

&
red
the
woof

red
the
woof

&
black
the
warp

red
the
woof

&
black
the
warp

black
the
warp

&
red
the
woof

black
the
warp

&
red
the
woof

tight

tight
the
string

of
the
harp

he
was
play-
ing

tight

tight
the
song

he
had
learn-
'd

to
in-
dite

tight

tight
the
string

of
the
harp

he
was
play-
ing

tight

tight
the
song

he
had
made

his
bas-
ket

his
bas-
ket

was
wov-
en

of
words

his
bas-
ket

his
bas-
ket

was
wov-
en

of
words

his
words

were
wove
tight

as
a
bas-
ket

a
bas-
ket

his
bas-
ket

his
bas-
ket

was
wov-
en

of
words

what

was
the
song

that
his
heart

was
in-
dit-
ing

his
heart

was
in-
dit-
ing

the
song

of
his

love

what

was
the
song

that
his
heart

was
in-
dit-
ing

?

his
heart

was
in-
dit-
ing

his
love

94

what

was
the
love

that
his
heart

was
in-
dit-
ing
?

a
love

a
love

a
mys-
ter-
i
ous

love

what
was
the
love

that
his
heart

was
in-
dit-
ing
?

a
love

a
mys-
ter-
i-
ous

love

95

black

black
the
warp

tight

tight
the
string

red

red
the
woof

of
my
love

of
my
love

black

black
the
warp

tight

tight
the
string

red

red
the
woof

of
my
love

a
sweet
wind

a
sweet
wind

blows

from
the
south

(but
my
love

is
far

a-
way)

a
sweet
wind

a
sweet
wind

blows

from
the
south

(but
my
heart

sings

well-
a-
day)

IV.

all
dreams

one
dream

all
mes-
sage

one
mes-
sage

all
mes-
sage

one
mes-
sage

all
dreams

one
dream

all
dreams

all
dreams

one
dream

one
dream

all
dreams

all
dreams

one
dream

one
dream

the
seas

the
seas

the
sea

the
sea

the
seas

the
seas

the
sea

the
sea

sea-
sons

&
sea-
sons

sea-
sons

&
sea-
sons

the
seas

the
seas

the
sea

all
dreams

one
dream

all
dreams

one
dream

      the
      sea

the
sea-
sons

      the
      sea

the
sea-
sons

      the
      sea

the
sea

the
sea

the
sea

the
sea

(the
sea

in
its

sea-
sons)

(the
sea

in
its

sea-
sons)

the
sea

the
sea

the
sea

the
sun

the
sun

the
sea

the
sun

the
sun

the
sea

(the
sea

in
its

sea
sons)

(the
sun

in
its

sea-
sons)

the
sea

the
sea

the
sea

these
              the
are
              sun
the
              the
sea-
              sun
sons

of
              the
sun
              sea

&
              the
sea
              sea

these
              the
              sun

are
              the
the
              sun
sea-
sons
              the
of
              sea
sun
              the
&
              sea
sea

the
sun

the
sun

the
sea

the
sea

the
sun

the
sun

the
sea

the
sea

that
ev-
'ry

span-
gle

dap-
pl-
'd

ban-
gle

sing
sing

sing
sing

that
ev-
'ry

span-
gle

dap-
pl-
'd

ban-
gle

sing

sing

sing

the
sun

the
sun

is
on

the
sea

the
sun

the
sun

is
on

the
sea

the
sun

the
sun

is
on

the
sea

the
sun

is
on

the
sea

that
ev-
'ry

span-
gle

dap-
pl-
'd

ban-
gle

sing
sing

sing
sing

that
ev-
'ry

span-
gle

dap-
pl-
'd

ban-
gle

sing

sing

sing

the
word

the
word

is

a

fly-
ing

bird

(a
bird

a
bird

a
bird)

the
word

the
word

is

a

fly-
ing

bird:

a
bird

a
bird

a
bird

V.

steer
your
course

steer
your
course

by
this

wheel

by
this

wheel

steer
your
course

steer
your
course

by
this

wheel

by
this

wheel

by
this

wheel

by
this

wheel

steer
your
course

steer
your
course

by
this

wheel

by
this

wheel

steer

your

course

the
sea

the
sea

(the
bos-
om

of
the
sea)

the
sea

the
sea

(the
bos-
om

of
the
sea)

bos-
om

bos-
om

(the
bos-
om

of
the
sea)

the
sea

the
sea

(the
bos-
om

of
the
sea)

the
sea

the
sea

(the
bos-
om

of
the
sea)

bos-
om

bos-
om

(the
bos-
om

of
the
sea)

bos-
om

bos-
om

(the
bos-
om

of
the

sea)

if
i

were
a
bird

i
would
fly

i
would
fly

out
ov-
er

the
sea

out
ov-
er

the
sea

if
i

were
a
bird

i
would
fly

i
would
fly

out
ov-
er

the
sea

out
ov-
er

the
sea

out
ov-
er

the
sea

out
ov-
er

the
sea

i
would
fly

i
would
fly

i
would
fly

out
ov-
er

the
sea

out
ov-
er

the
sea

i
would
fly

i
would
fly

i
would
fly

the
far-
off

cit-
y

the
far-
off

cit-
y

light
the
light

on
the

far-
off

cit-
y

the
far-
off

cit-
y

the
far-
off

cit-
y

the
light

the
light

the
light

110

if
i

were
a
bird

if
i

were
a
bird

i
would
fly

i
would
fly

(to
the
far-
off

cit-
y)

if
i

were
a
bird

if
i

were
a
bird

i
would
fly

i
would
fly

i
would
fly

out
ov-
er

the
sea

out
ov-
er

the
sea

i
would
fly

i
would
fly

i
would
fly

out
ov-
er

the
sea

out
ov-
er

the
sea

i
would
fly

i
would
fly

i
would
fly

the
light

the
light

is
on

the
sea

the
light

is
on

the
sea

the
light

the
light

is
on

the
sea

the
light

is
on

the
sea

the cit- y	the cit- y
the cit- y	the cit- y
the far- off	the far- off
cit- y	cit- y
(the light	(the light
is on	is on
the sea)	the sea)

the
light

the
light

the
sea

the
sea

(the
light

the
light

the
sea

the
sea)

VI.

the
slow-
est

the
slow-
est

of
move-
ments

of
move-
ments

a-
long

the
sur-
face

of
the

sea

the
slow-
est

the
slow-
est

of
move-
ments

of
move-
ments

a-
long

the
sur-
face

of
the

sea

be-
cause

the
changes

be-
cause

the
changes

of
sea

are
the
changes

of
mu-
sic

be-
cause

the
changes

be-
cause

the
changes

of
sea

are
the
changes

of
mu-
sic

the
slow-
est

of
move-
ments

the
slow-
est

of
move-
ments

is
on

the
sea

is
on

the
sea

as
oce-
an

as
oce-
an

re-
flects

the
sky

the
ci-
ties

of
man

the
cit-
y

(of
God)

as
oce-
an

as
oce-
an

re-
flects

the
sky

the
cit-
ies

of
man

(of
God)

what
cur-
rent

what
cur-
rent

is
un-
der

the
sea

what
cur-
rent

what
cur-
rent

is
un-
der

the
sea

cold
cur-
rent

warm
cur-
rent

smooth
cur-
rent

strong
cur-
rent

(cur-
rent)

what
cur-
rent

is
un-
der

the
sea

?

the
sun
smiles

the
sea
smiles

the
moon
smiles

the
sea
smiles

light

light

on
the
sea

(on
the
sea)

light

light

(on
the
sea)

the
sky

is

one

the
air

is

one

the
sea

the
sea

the
sea

is

one

the
sky

is
one

the
air

is
one

the
sea

the
sea

the
sea

the
sea

may
reach

the
sea

may
reach

but
on-
ly

the
sky

but-
on-
ly

the
sky

the
sea

may
reach

the
sea

may
reach

but
on-
ly

the
sky

(leans
down)

the
sea

may
reach

the
sea

may
reach

but
on-
ly

the
sky

but
on-
ly

the
sky

the
sea

may
reach

the
sea

may
reach

but
on-
ly

the
sky

(leans
down)

the
dark-
ness

the
dark-
ness

(the
face

of
the

sea)

the
dark-
ness

the
dark-
ness

(the
face

of
the

sea)

VII.

how
still

how
still

(&
the
domes

how
still)

how
still

how
still

is
the

sea

how
still

how
still

(&
the
domes

how
still)

how
still

the
wind-
less

sea

the	the
sea	sea
the	the
sea	sea
the	the
air	air
the	the
air	air
the	the
sky	sky
the	the
sky	sky
the	the
sky	sky

the
air

is
a

gi-
ant

who
holds

his
hand

be-
tween

the
sea

&

the
sky

the
air

is
a

gi-
ant:

he
holds

his
hand

be-
tween

the
sea

&

the
sky

the
dream-
ing

dream-
ing

sea

re-
gards

the
smil-
ing

sky

the
dream-
ing

dream-
ing

sea

re-
gards

the
smil-
ing

sky

the
dream-
ing

sea

the
smil-
ing

sky

the
dream-
ing

dream-
ing

sea

the
dream-
ing

sea

the
smil-
ing

sky

the
dream-
ing

dream-
ing

sea

(the
sea

may
reach

the
sea

may
reach)

the
sky

looks
down

looks

down

(the
sea

may
reach

the
sea

may
reach)

the
sky

looks
down

looks

down

if
i

were
a
bird

if
i

were
a
bird

i
would
fly

to
the
ends

of
the
sea

if
i

were
a
bird

if
i

were
a
bird

i
would
fly

to
the
ends

of
the
sea

the
sea

the
sea

the
sky

the
sky

the
sky

the
sky

the
sea

the
sea

the
sea

the
sea

the
sky

the
sky

the
sky

the
sky

the
sea

the
sea

the
domes

the
domes

are
still

are
still

the
sea

the
sea

is
still

the
domes

are
still

the
sea

is
still

the
air

is
still

is
still

(the
domes

are
still

the
sea

is
still)

the
air

is
still

is
still

what

are
the
cur-
rents

un-
der

the
sea

what

are
the
cur-
rents

un-
der

the
sea

(the
sea

is
a
dream-
ing

sea)

what

are
the
cur-
rents

un-
der

the
sea

what

are
the
cur-
rents

un-
der

the
sea

(the
sea
's

a
yearn-
ing

sea)

the
sea

may
reach

the
sea

may
reach

(the
sky

looks
down

looks
down)

the
sea

may
reach

the
sea

may
reach

(the
sky

looks
down

looks
down)

what

are
the
cur-
rents

un-
der

the
sea

(the
sea

is
a
dream-
ing

sea)

what

are
the
cur-
rents

un-
der

the
sea

(the
sea-
's

a
yearn-
ing

sea)

the	the
air	air
the	the
air	air
the	the
sky	sky
the	the
sky	sky
the	the
sea	sea
the	the
sea	sea
the	the
sea	sea

ABSTRACT POEM

red	red	black	red
red	red	black	red
black	black	blue	black
black	black		black
black	black	black	black
black	black	black	black
blue	blue	blue	blue

Orig. ca. 1965. First publ.
in *Retort* Vol. 42, # 3, 1967

ABLE CHARLIE BAKER DANCE

a-	bak-	char-	dance
ble	er	lie	
bak-	a-	a-	a-
er	ble	ble	ble
char-	char-	bak-	bak-
lie	lie	er	er
a-	bak-	char-	dance
ble	er	lie	
char-	char-	bak-	bak-
lie	lie	er	er
bak-	a-	a-	a-
er	ble	ble	ble
a-	bak-	char-	dance
ble	er	lie	
bak-	a-	a-	a-
er	ble	ble	ble
dance	dance	dance	char-
			lie

Orig. 1967. Ed. by Emil Antonucci with
Tarasque Press, East Markham [GB], 1971

a-ble	bak-er	char-lie	dance
dance	dance	dance	char-lie
bak-er	a-ble	a-ble	a-ble

a-ble	bak-er	char-lie	dance
char-lie	char-lie	bak-er	bak-er
dance	dance	dance	char-lie

a-ble	bak-er	char-lie	dance
dance	dance	dance	char-lie
char-lie	char-lie	bak-er	bak-er

a- ble	bak- er	char- lie	dance
a- ble	bak- er	char- lie	dance
bak- er	a- ble	a- ble	a- ble
a- ble	bak- er	char- lie	dance
a- ble	bak- er	char- lie	dance
char- lie	char- lie	bak- er	bak- er
a- ble	bak- er	char- lie	dance
a- ble	bak- er	char- lie	dance
dance	dance	dance	char- lie

a- ble	bak- er	char- lie	dance
a- ble	bak- er	char- lie	dance
a- ble	bak- er	char- lie	
			dance
a- ble	bak- er	char- lie	dance
bak- er	a- ble	a- ble	a- ble
a- ble	bak- er	char- lie	
			dance
a- ble	bak- er	char- lie	dance
char- lie	char- lie	bak- er	bak- er
a- ble	bak- er	char- lie	
			dance

a- ble	bak- er	char- lie	dance
dance	dance	dance	char- lie
a- ble	bak- er	char- lie	dance
a- ble	bak- er	char- lie	dance
bak- er	a- ble	a- ble	a- ble
bak- er	a- ble	a- ble	a- ble
a- ble	bak- er	char- lie	dance
char- lie	char- lie	bak- er	bak- er
char- lie	char- lie	bak- er	bak- er

a- ble	bak- er	char- lie	dance
			char- lie
dance	dance	dance	lie
			char- lie
dance	dance	dance	lie

A PROBLEM IN DESIGN

what if
you like
to draw
big flowers,

but what
if some
sage has
told you
that
there is
nothing
more
beautiful

nothing
more
beautiful

than a
straight
line
?

what should
you draw:
big flowers?
straight lines?

i think
you should
draw

Orig. 1958, 1961, 1969. This
version first publ. in "R. L.: Fables",
ed. by Emil Antonucci with
Journeyman Press, New York 1970

big flowers
big flowers

big flowers
big flowers

big flowers
big flowers

big flowers
big flowers

until
they become
a straight
line.

THE ANGEL
AND THE LITTLE OLD LADY

an angel
appeared to
a little old
lady

& said:

would you
like a
wish?

for my
grand-daughter,
said the little
old lady:

that she grow
up to be a
beautiful young
lady

& marry a
nice young
man

two wishes,
said the angel,

would you
like another?

whatever other
good thing you
can think of,

said the little
old lady

Orig. 1969. First publ. by Emil
Antonucci with *Journeyman Press*,
New York 1969

the girl grew up
to be a beautiful
young lady

& married a
nice young man

after a year or
so, a child was
born to them

(the angel's
idea)

- - -

now the old
lady was
quite a bit
older:

the angel
appeared
to her again
& said:

would you
like a
wish?

for the
child, she
said

that he grow
up to be a
handsome
young man

& marry

a nice
young girl

two wishes
said the angel,

would you
like another?

whatever other
good thing
you can think
of,

said the little
old lady

SHEPHERD'S CALENDAR

1.

move	move	rocks	move
ment	ment	like	ment
of	of	sheep	of
sheep	sheep		rocks
move	move	sheep	move
ment	ment	like	ment
of	of	rocks	of
rocks	rocks		rocks

2.

the	the
sheep's	bell's
bell	tongue
the	the
sheep's	sheep's
tongue	tongue
the	the
sheep's	sheep's
bell	tongue
the	the
bell's	bell's
tongue	tongue

Orig. 1969. Publ. in *The New York Quarterly* # 1, Winter 1970. Also *Furthermore Press,* Lyndonville, VT., 1983

3.

the	the
sheep	boy
eats	waits

the	the
boy	sheep
waits	eats

the	the
sheep	boy
eat	waits

the	the
boy	sheep
waits	eat

4.

sheep	boy
wan	throws
ders	stones

boy	sheep
throws	wan
stone	der

sheep	sheep
wan	wan
der	ders

boy	boy
throws	throws
stones	stone

5.

bleat	bleat
lamb	sheep
bleat	bleat
sheep	lamb
sheep	sheep
eats	eat
sheep	sheep
eat	eats

6.

drift	sink
shad	sun
ow	
drift	drift
sheep	shad
	ow
drift	sink
shad	sun
ow	
drift	drift
sheep	sheep

SEVEN EPISODES

every day when joe walked
down the street
he would meet mrs. macluski
coming down the other way
"hello mrs. macluski"
joe would say
"hello joe" mrs. macluski
would reply

one day it wasn't mrs. macluski
coming down the street
it was the queen

"hello your highness" said joe
as usual
"hello joe" said the queen
"how's things?"

Orig. betw. 1945 and 1979. Publ. in
"R. L.: Episodes/Episoden", ed. by Robert
Butman with *pendo-verlag*, Zürich 1983

all i want
is for my son
to get married

what did you say, mummy?

nothing, son,
nothing at all, i was just
thinking

oh, all right, then,
mumsey

all i want
in the whole bleeding
world

is for my son
to get married

when i play house
i don't play
either the poppa
or the mama

it's more
as though i was playing
i was
the house

mother
er
if
we

don't
move
out
of
blens-
ville

i'll
pro-
bab-
ly

shoot
my-
self,

moth-
er

do
you
know
that

?

the angel came to him & said

 i'm sorry, mac, but
we talked it over
in heaven
& you're going

to have to live
a thousand years

it was only when the dentist
talked to her about life
that she realized she had one

a dog walked wearily
from one side of the town to the other
saying to himself

"i'll find a cat to chase
today or i'll never leave the house
again"

TRACTATUS I–II

I

he was determined this time not to write about anything, to keep
as far away from any possible subject as he could and just to keep
going, to include or to exclude whatever came to mind, not
necessarily to lead it in, not necessarily to leave it out: to let
things rise to his consciousness, to be examined briefly, and let
fall again or invited to enter. he knew these places well, these ups
and downs, these ins and outs, he saw them as he'd see a
building, an old and quite familiar building. he ran around it
through the day, and all through the night, in dreams, he was
mounting and descending its well-worn stairs. as a watcher, he
would watch things rise, or as an actor, he himself would climb,
and fall. (one memory jarred with another: one would collide
with another.) no, he would not approach a single subject: not
one of the many that played through his mind through the day.
(there was a process of knitting going on: the form of the
stitches was more important than the color of the yarn.) to keep
going: to turn one wheel after another: a large one after a small
one, a small one after a large one, until all wheels were
spinning, innumerable wheels spinning, and spinning, perhaps,
within the circumference of a single, very large wheel; a single
globe.

he would not stop now to describe the globe: describe a
globe: all globes except for their sizes were much alike. he would
not attempt to describe a moment of something moving, of
something regretted, desired, lost. the moments were clear in his
memory, but he had not a word for one of them.

even as the rains fell, the times fell, the moments fell. the
moments dropped as from a moving cloud. they intensified as
they neared a particular point, and then, again, they diminished.
even as the rains spoke, the times spoke: articulations just
beyond the realm of consciousness. there were accumulations
and releases; releases and re-accumulation. whatever was
scattered, was gathered; whatever was gathered, was scattered.
no time stood for long; no moment endured forever. each
moment proclaimed the business of the moment. in every
moment, hidden or manifest, there was a possible fulfillment.

Orig. 1971. Publ. in
Dryad # 9/10, 1972

each moment made its demand, and each its offer. each was a sphere; each held to its sphericity a moment.

the realm he lived in was not a realm of earth: could hardly even be called a realm of sky: the realm of mind was neither here nor there: it knew its own true north, its own true west. its storms were not land storms, were not sky storms, were not like storms at sea. its rains fell in their season, not earth's seasons. the realm of mind: united and divided: united within itself; divided against itself; united within themselves; divided against themselves.

the	the	the	the
red	blue	red	blue
(grow-	(grow-	(grow	(grow
ing	ing	ing	ing
dark)	red)	blue)	dark)
con	con	con	con
front	front	front	front
ed	ed	ed	ed
the	the	the	the
blue	red	blue	red

no: that was clear. there would be no writing them into his book. they were a race unto themselves, a law unto themselves: a race without law, a law without table. they knew each other, and knew their ways. they understood the changes. they understood all things, in fact, as though the whole pattern had been played to them in music. they knew at each moment what music would be next.

they knew (within the tribe) what things mattered and what did not. and yet their tribe was not a tribe, their tribes, not tribes. they were outcasts of all the tribes, and yet they hung together better than tribes. each knew the other's sleeplessness: each knew the other's hunger.

their language was no, not born of desperation or despair. it was born of humility, born almost of weariness: but born of humility, born of weariness, it was born strong, and born to stay.

one thing they knew: they could descend no further; they could go down no further and yet live. they lived on the margins of the day, they lived on the margins of the night. they were almost sleepless; they were never idle. but even their idleness was a chain: there was no freedom in their vigil. no freedom, and no tears. no freedom, and little laughter. some laughter, yes. no tears. they had left off crying.

II

even at the bottom of the sea, the presence of the sun at the surface made itself felt

to walk along the street and not become enmeshed in their faces

an upstairs world and a downstairs world

the heroes were the ones with the straight faces

all the minor characters were twisted by comparison

one experience vibrated for days, for months, for years

others which seemed important at the time were forgotten in a moment

the sounds were familiar and foreign at once

shapeless lights in the inner world

162

precision of movement, precision of reflection

the scene was a changing scene, the characters, too, changed from moment to moment

morning had innocence; the afternoon, majesty

they woke and slept, woke and slept; they knew their own times, their own seasons

there were times, single moments when the speech of one would cut through the air to reach another

if the sea was calm in this bay, it was calm in the bay that faced it

the afternoon had a tone of its own

it pervaded the hills, the trees, the sea (the sunlight)

it stood as a dancer might, with all its weight balanced at a single point

it imposed a silence

afternoons of memory: boats in the bay, the quayside buildings

in actuality, all was as actual as the eye

a stretched white cord from which a tone might vibrate

sketchings of that ideal place toward which all hopes aspired

the sea imposed its limitations on movement

move: but move so, in such paths, at such speed

the sea would not be hurried, the sun would not be hurried: the clouds stood as though quite still, and would not hurry

all through the afternoon, the roosters called, long tones, long cries, not seeming to require an answer

(the afternoon itself designed a suit of armor for the hero)

the hero entered the lists bearing emblems of life: his shield emblazoned with emblems of the living

ONE ISLAND

Orig. 1975. Publ. in *Hanging Loose*
29, Winter 1976–77

I

cir
cle

of
brown

cir
cle

of
blue

cir
cle

of
brown

cir
cle

of
blue

cir
cle

of
earth

cir
cle

of
earth

cir
cle

of
sea

cir
cle

of
sea

cir   cir
cle   cle

of   of
brown   earth

cir   cir
cle   cle

of   of
brown   earth

cir   cir
cle   cle

of   of
blue   sea

cir
cle

of
blue

com
ing

of
dark

com
ing

of
dark

com
ing

of
light

com
ing

of
light

com
ing

of
dark

com
ing

of
dark

com
ing

of
light

earth   earth
cir   cir
cle   cle

earth   earth
cir   cir
cle   cle

sea   sea
cir   cir
cle   cle

sea   sea
cir   cir
cle   cle

```
brown          earth
brown          earth

blue           earth
blue           earth


brown          sea
brown
               sea

blue           sea
blue
```

pres
ence

of
light

pres
ence

of
light

pres
ence

of
dark

pres
ence

of
dark

pres
ence

of
dark

pres
ence

of
dark

pres
ence

of
light

dark	land
dark	land
light	sea
light	sea

dark	land
dark	land
light	sea
light	

leaf   leaf
sound   sound

leaf   leaf
sound   sound

wave   wave
sound   sound

wave   wave
sound   sound

land
smell

land
smell

land
smell

land
smell

sea
smell

sea
smell

sea
smell

sea
smell

com
ing

of
dark

com
ing

of
dark

com
ing

of
light

com
ing

of
light

com
ing

of
dark

com
ing

of
dark

com
ing

of
light

II

black	red
rocks	earth
black	red
rocks	earth
green	red
leaves	earth
green	red
leaves	earth
black	black
rocks	rocks
black	black
rocks	rocks
green	green
leaves	leaves

light   light

cuts   cuts

shad   shad
ow   ow

shad   shad
ow   ow

cuts   cuts

light   light

stone
shad
ow

leaf
shad
ow

stone
shad
ow

leaf
shad
ow

leaf
shad
ow

stone
shad
ow

leaf
shad
ow

stone
shad
ow

land
wind

land
wind

sea
wind

sea
wind

sea
wind

sea
wind

land
wind

land
wind

hill
shad
ow

hill
shad
ow

cloud
shad
ow

cloud
shad
ow

hill
shad
ow

hill
shad
ow

cloud
shad
ow

cloud
shad
ow

land   sea
cir   cir
cle   cle

land   sea
cir   cir
cle   cle

sea   land
cir   cir
cle   cle

sea   land
cir   cir
cle   cle

leaf   leaf
sound   sound

leaf   leaf
sound   sound

wave   wave
sound   sound

wave   wave
sound   sound

goat's   goat's
cry   cry

goat's   goat's
cry   cry

bird's   bird's
cry   cry

bird's   bird's
cry   cry

is
land

is
land

one
is
land

one
is
land

is
land

one
is
land

one
rock

one
sea

TIGER

a tiger
is like a
butterfly,
thought
the
tiger,

here today,
gone tomorrow

he is like a
bird — a hawk,
forever
vigilant

he is even
a little
like an
elephant,

ponderous
& basically
gentle.

not too
gentle,

said a
younger
tiger.

Orig. ca. 1981. First publ. in
"R. L.: Fables/Fabeln", *pendo-verlag*,
1983. Also *Furthermore Press*,
Passumpsic VT., 1983

184

i only meant it

as a metaphor,
said the old one,

a tiger is like
a number of
things.

21   PAGES

Orig. 1982. Publ.
by *pendo-verlag*,
Zürich 1984

Searching for you, but if there's no one, what am I searching
for? Still you. Some sort of you. Not for myself? Am I
you? Need I search for me? For myself? Is my self you? I
know: Self. Is that you? Is it me? Why search? I seem to
be built to. Search dog, search hound: built that way. That's
me. I know me. Do I know you? Do I at all? Have I had
some signs or flashes? Any clues? Was that a clue? What
one? Any one I can have had, or think I've had, or imagine
myself to have had, in times past or even now as I ask. Is asking
a clue? Is wanting to know what you are, who you are, any
proof that you are, that you're there? Wasting time: I might
be using it for what? What use it for when all I want to know
is where you are. I go on searching, I was born for that. I
don't remember being born. What makes me sure I was? Or
that I was for anything.

Time for distraction. I'll count to 150. Count to 150 by
threes. I'll start at 150 and work back by threes and fours:
147, 143, 136, 133, 129, 126, 122, 119. Tedium. I'll
return to the search, cross-legged, silencing the mind. Do I
have legs? My body has: I can cross & uncross them. I
cross them now and sit with – is it mine? – my spine erect.
I sit with spine erect & stare, not fiercely, into the dark. I am
searching again, as I always am, as I always do. One way as
good as another.

Looking straight ahead, not fiercely, with only one object in
mind. No objects. Looking straight ahead and waiting.
Waiting not searching. Searching & waiting. How do I know
what it is? I know. I know because I keep doing it, waiting
& searching for what, for whom? How will I know when I've
found it, found him, found you? How wouldn't I know?
How could I expect not to know what I'd found when I found
you? Do I just go on searching, looking, waiting? Do I find
you? Do you find me? Will I know I've been found? How
wouldn't I know.

How would I not know what I was looking for? But I don't. But I do. I've been doing it for so long I must know something. Not much. Not enough to hold onto. A vague idea. Do I know what I'm not looking for? I do. Do I know what I am? I don't. Would I know you if I saw you? Would I know you if you came toward me down the street? Staring into the dark at night, would I know you if I saw you staring back? Not staring, looking. Would I know your face if I saw it? Would I think it was you? Have I seen you before? Do I know, do you know where it was, when it was? Is there any chance I'd remember?

Something I remember about standing in the rain, on the street, upright, of course, and in the driving rain. Not driving, a vertical downpour. Night and under a light in the downpour of rain. Did I ask any questions then? Did I see a face? I was absolutely alone on the street. Alone. I was part of the rain. Not part of the rain, part of the moment the rain was about. I knew where I was. I knew what I was doing. I knew what the rain was doing. There was nothing particular about it to recall.

I remember other times, some only in dreams, times I'd recognize if I saw them again. Times of things coming together, working together. What do any of these things have to do with you? Why do I remember them? Why do I sift through them? I do, but not because I know what they may hold. If there's anything they hold.

Times of feeling you were there, that you were close. A hall, a corridor: walking down a corridor, the damp stone walls, a smell of dampness, cold, but a feeling of what? That I wasn't alone? That someone was near, not visible, but near me, that someone was there. Who, though?

Or in a dream, in a house, a low sort of house, a cabin by the river, wide window looking out on the river. House very steady. River moving slowly. An in-between light, neither dark or light. Twilight. Between night and morning. No, evening and night. Between evening & night. I'm inside the house, cross-legged, not crossed, just sitting on the floor, looking out at the river, dark river, grey light. I'm not alone. Or I am, but not alone like now. I'm waiting, not waiting. I'm there.

When I'm there, you're there; when I'm not, you're not. If I'm not here, I'm waiting. Try it again: when you're here, I'm here too, and when you're not, then I'm not. Where am I then, when you're not here? I'm nowhere. What am I doing nowhere? Waiting. I'm sitting in (what we'll call) nowhere, looking into the dark, and waiting.

I ought to be able to say it better than that. But how? By not trying? I'll try not to try. I'll try to say it the way it is, the way I see it. But I won't try too hard. Trying too hard gets me off the track. I know where I am now. I know I can get some part of it said. I can, if I don't try too hard.

Wake up & wait. Lie down & wait. Sit up again & wait. All in the dark now. No way of telling day from night. Do I expect to hear a sound? Do I expect to hear a voice? See a light? A dim one? A bright one? See a face? I sit up. I'm alert. Do I know what to expect?

I don't know what to expect, but I do know what I'm doing. I know what it feels like to be doing what I'm doing. I feel like a sentinel. I'm on guard duty. I don't know what to expect. Friend or enemy? Friend. I'm waiting for a friend. Someone who may become a friend. May turn out to be one.

Why wait? Why watch? What better have I to do? Have I anything else to do? Might sing. Sing in this darkness? How would I hear your voice if I were singing? Might count. No counting. Count very softly. No.

189

My childhood was a happy one.   I was this.   I was that.   My parents adored me: I remember that.   I wanted for nothing. I was fully supplied.   Practically, there was nothing I might have asked for.   I didn't ask.   I didn't often.   If I asked, I was given.   If I sought, I found.   So much for the early years. I can hardly recall them.

School: I went to one in the country, a small school with a single master.   I must have done well enough in my studies; I remember no rewards, and no punishments.   Or few.   When the master spoke to the class, he seemed to be talking to the other students; I never felt he was talking to me.   As I reached the age of puberty, the whole experience came to an end.   We must have moved to the city then, and my schooling was over.

Schooling was over & my waiting began.   I'm sure that's about when it started.   It must have begun very quietly.   I didn't notice it begin.   I realized I was doing something new.   I didn't know I was waiting.   I knew I was doing something almost all the time, some new thing.   Something that joined one day to the next.   I never wondered what I was doing anymore.   I knew I was doing that thing.

That thing, but not that I was waiting.   I was simply continuing.   I was going from day to day with just one purpose: to remain in the state I was in.   What state?   A state of alert. But alertness for what?   I hadn't even the beginning of a notion at that point.

Like a prisoner, waiting for a reprieve, counting the days, not counting, not knowing what to count or why to count it, waiting for one thing, one moment, one event.   I didn't feel like a prisoner, but I was waiting like one; doing nothing else but waiting.

Or like a child, a foetus, I mean, waiting in darkness, warm or lukewarm darkness to be born.   I was waiting for things to start happening.   I was waiting to begin to be.

190

Or like waiting for a letter that doesn't arrive.   That will arrive, but hasn't yet.   It will, or it won't.   There's nothing you can do to bring it along.   Can you think about it all the time? You can't.   But can you forget it?

I do think about it all the time.   I don't.   But I don't forget. Always somewhere in the back of my mind, up front, right here, right there.   Candle flame glowing in some dark corner.   Vigil light.   Or a window on the dark.   You see nothing from inside.   There's just the possibility of seeing.

Like waiting in a sunless valley, in a narrow pass between two mountains, waiting for a ray of light.   Families live there all year around.   Never see the sun.   Never stop waiting.   Night follows day, but sun never falls directly into the chasm.   Always a shadow, always a cloud.

When the wind blows, I listen to the wind; when the rain falls, I listen to the rain.   I sift through the sounds to see if there's another.   To see if there's one I can cling to & call my own. Nothing so far.

I open my eyes in the dark and see darkness.   I close my eyes, even in the light, and see darkness.   All the same darkness. Almost the same.   Light comes and goes, but the darkness stays.   Almost always the same.   A fairly steady darkness. One you can count on.   Almost.

Sounds come and go, but the silence remains.   Silence, unbroken, except for occasional noises.   The substance is silence, dark silence.   There's always some stir, some light, some sound, then they stop, and there's only dark silence.

I wait in the dark, in the rain, no sound but the rain.   Waiting, not waiting, doing nothing but waiting.   Does the darkness move?   Does the silence move?   They don't, and neither do I. Are they waiting?   I have no way of knowing.

I don't know if it waits, but I think it moves.   The darkness does.   There are masses of it, masses in it, and they shift.   A silent moving of force against force, mass against mass.   A feeling of chaos, too.   Not total chaos.

Movement of dark things in darkness, looking for order. Looking for some relief from total, all but total, chaos.   Dark things moving in darkness, trying to find some kind of adjustment, some form of order.   I look into the dark and see darkness, no more light than at the half-imagined edges of these dark objects.   Darkness made up of objects slowly turning, jostling and turning, slowly turning, trying to discover some kind of accord.

I'm not really waiting, I'm watching.   Watching while waiting. Looking into the darkness and watching it move.   Watching the movement of dark things in darkness: a push from the left, a push from the right; a struggling movement up from below. Did I say it was chaos?   It isn't chaos.   There's some kind of action in it, some kind of will.

Is it my will?   I don't think it's my will.   It's just the will of the things that are moving.   Things, or whatever they are.

Sections of darkness.   Ice floes of darkness, afloat in the sea. Drifting, turning, colliding.   Smacking up against each other, breaking, turning, drifting.   Dark whales at swim in the night sea.   They swim toward each other.   Toward each other, and away.

Dark dolphins leaping above the dark sea.   Purposive movement. What purpose?   Dark dolphins, just before dawn, adip in the night-sea.   Dark rocks, dark dolphin, dark wave.

No, it isn't like that.   All dark, but it isn't like that. Darker, more solid, less budge.   Not budgeless, but not so much moving around.   Not smacking together.   A bump, a thud. No smacking.   A black-curtained scene, hardly moving most of the time.

192

Dark, like a black cat.   Dark and shining.   It has its dormant
times, its active times.   Cat nap & cat nip.   Sleeping and
leaping.   First one, then the other.   Active dark, passive
dark.   Sometimes you watch, sometimes you wait.   Looking
into the dark do I see a black cat?   I just see the dark, but it
changes.

Like this & like that.   Like a cat.   Like a cloud.   Light cloud,
phosphorescent, but only lightly phosphorescent in a field. Light
cloud, afloat in dark field.   Light, barely visible, inner light of
light cloud, phosphorescent, afloat, hardly moving, not adrift,
not standing, afloat, hardly moving in night dark field.

I found work at last: watch-maker's assistant.   Clock-maker's,
rather.   I brought him the sand.   He fashioned the globes &
measured the hours.   I brought him miniscule white cups of
coffee too: not every hour, by any stretch, and not often even
on time.   But it was a job, a means of livelihood of sorts, that
didn't interfere with my real work, my continuing preoccupation.
Or hardly ever did.   He didn't like dreaming; he did like the
sound of feet running.   What he got in the hours, days, nights
and what must have been months I was with him was a little of
each.

Some running, some standing & dreaming.   More running.
More standing, sitting, or leaning against the door-frame,
obviously dreaming.   It was, as I've said, a livelihood; not
rich, not an inch above subsistence, but enough to let me
continue in my chosen way.

My way at that time was ill-defined, but pursuable. There were
nights, midnights, when I could sit up alone on the cot he'd
assigned me, eyes closed, eyes open, to watch, to wait, hardly
breathing, fully alert, as alert as I could be, to any change
in the dark's part light but mostly dark configurations. This
watching might go on for hours, one or two, one, two or three,
sometimes till just a moment or two before dawn, till at last I'd
lie down again for an hour's sleep. The longer the long night's
watching, the slower the next day's running for sand and coffee.
The less dreams by night, the more by day: standing, sitting,
listing, leaning, mooning about on the master's time and
premises. The situation was bound to end one day, gently or
abruptly by mutual accord, and before many days, weeks,
months had gone by, it did.

The situation ended, that is, the job did, but not for a moment
my underlying pursuit; if anything it intensified in the months of
physical fast & privation that followed. The cot was gone, but
the world had become my pallet. Wherever I slept or slept not
was now my preserve. I've forgotten the number and kinds of
places I found: whatever was shelter. I didn't need much.
The weather was clement and I'd grown accustomed to the
rigors of uncushioned existence. My observatory powers in the
meantime had grown keener. I could see in the dark. I could
see much further into the dark than before.

I saw more then than I had before, and more than I see now, in
my present state. My fallen state. But I'm getting ahead of my
story, if that's what it is.

My fallen state, if that's what it is. My dark night of the soul, if
that's what it is. My long night's waiting, if that's what it is. I
saw a lot more then, on those nights of sleeping, not sleeping
under bridges, sleeping, not sleeping on benches, under
trees, in barn or on church step than I'm seeing now. No
matter. I continue to watch.

I continue to watch, & that's what counts. What counts, if anything does. Something does, but the question I more often ask myself is who counts it? Do I? I do. But does anyone else? Does anyone else in the universe count what happens? Does anyone else in the universe know what matters? Does anyone care, I mean, personally care? Ah, well, why get into that, as long as I do.

And I do. Seem to. Seem to want to know what's going on. From moment to moment. Why it's going on. What counts, from moment to moment. I want to know. Seem to. Seem to want to know. Seem to want to know what it's all, or even, what any small part of it's about.

Image follows image. Image flows into image, not one stays long enough to describe. White writing on black. White web in dark night. Pale sliver of moon appears and disappears. Where is the energy? Where is the push?

The white is drifting about in the black. Appears and disappears. Forms and disintegrates, quietly. Forms, drifts and disappears. White is a light foam. The black is the sea.

Black lives, rises, expands, subsides. Black has energy, black has its law. White forms at random. The black has a plan. Black grows like a tree. Black moves like the sea.

There are nights, there are times when there's no white at all, or it's so dim, green or grey you would hardly call it present: just a film, just a mist, the memory of a glow. But the black, the black sea, the black tree, is always there. Always growing, always living, always changing. Full of energy & on the move. But always there.

Should I watch the white? Should I watch the black? I look into the black and see the white moving before it. I look into the dark. I don't look into the light. The light disappears if I watch it. The dark remains.

An eye.   Do I see an eye?   Looking back at me in the dark.
It's like an eye.   Has a point, a pupil.   Flashes and disappears.
Flash, dim white flash.   I see the corner of the eyelid too.
Outer corner.   Nice line.   Two graceful curves, joined at the
corner.   Dim white.   Sometimes I see it.   Hardly, but see it.

Eye looking back.   Not fiercely, no.   But gently?   Intensely?
Just steadily from deep in the dark, like something in nature,
deep in the woods.

Or as though my own eye could see itself looking.   My eye
meets the eye in the dark.   The eye in the dark meets mine.   No
fire exchanged, just two quiet glances.

My eye.   Your eye.   Or even if it's mine & mine.   Why should
my eye look at your eye?   Why should yours look into mine?
Am I seeking out a glance, a look, in darkness?

Hundreds of eyes I've looked at and into: not just in the dark;
at every hour of the day.   Looking for what?   Some kind of
response?   Eyes of every ocular shape and color, and of every
degree of liveliness and flaccidity.   Some that weren't alive at
all.   Some that looked like exploding universes.

I worked for a while for an entrepreneur.   I brought him the
cardboard.   He cut out the forms.   I ran for the oil; he filled
the lamps.   At night his shadows moved across the screen.
Children in the audience screamed with delight, but I trembled.
After the first few evenings I didn't watch at all.   The works
were comedies mostly, but not for me.   Too many characters
beheaded, or almost beheaded.   Too many hard slaps delivered
to the jaw.

It wasn't the proper environment for me to grow in.   I told him
so, not knowing whether or not he would understand.   After a
number of days, nights, weeks, months, the arrangement came
to an end, and I was left on my own again, still waiting.

For you. For someone or something I'd recognize. A person, a moment. A sign you were there. Or had been; or were going to be, soon. Those comedies didn't help me at all. I was glad to be out in the dark where I could forget them.

Not that I ever forget a thing. It's all there, all I've done, all that's ever happened, is still there, somewhere in suspension. Waiting in the wings. Or riding above the tide. Above it, or below it. It's all there somewhere, it's just that I don't recall it. Never do, or seldom. Never try to call it to mind. Never try to replay the scene. Why should I? It's not in my interest.

Not in my interest because if I'm looking anywhere, I'm looking ahead. I'm looking toward some point, some vanishing point, or anyway, not yet visible point in the distance, in the future where something or someone I'd recognize would appear. (Where you would appear.)

Some person, some moment, some atmosphere, that I'd recognize as very much mine, would be there.

My person. My beloved, if you like; my sought-after-being, my remembered-one, would be there. The one I'd looked for, the one I'd sought without any clear idea of who he or she might be, of what he or she might look like, would appear.

Not, as I've said, that I had no idea. Not no idea; but no clear one. Not an idea I could hold well in mind. Far less an idea than a feeling, a dim, unfading area of light, a possibility as yet unfulfilled, a readiness to recognize, someone, something. You.

A readiness to recognize you; that's all I've brought, that's what I bring to the encounter.

I worked for a printer for a little while. I brought him the wood. He cut out the letters. He'd line them up and we'd smear them with ink. I brought him wine, too, and a handful of almonds every so often throughout the day. I don't know what his novels were about, but the work was peaceful. I'd have stayed with him forever if he hadn't been arrested. I was out for wine & almonds when the authorities arrived. The shop was empty when I returned. Letters and ink all over the floor.

Back to the streets, the parks, the quays. Back to standing and looking, watching, not watching the passersby. Looking for a face. A face in the crowd. A particular one that I'd recognize and in a particular way. Did I think I'd find it? Did I know I'd find it? I knew I was engaged in just one thing: in looking. Looking and looking.

And back to nights of looking, outward and in; not knowing which way I'm looking, but waiting and looking. Back to the night-watch. Day-watch & night-watch Dusk to dawn, dawn to dusk. Mid-day to midnight. I don't say I didn't tire: I did. I tired, but I didn't give up.

I didn't give up, because I couldn't. I didn't, because I was made to go on waiting. Made, put together, invented, born, for that single, singular purpose: to watch, to wait. There's no giving up on the thing you were made to do. There's no giving up on being who you are.

Not for me, anyway. There was no giving up on being who I was, & there's no giving up on it now. I'm into the business of doing what I'm doing, of being who I am, and of waiting for whomever it is that I am, & have always been, waiting for. Into it, I guess, because, for the moment, there's nowhere else I could be.

Or would much want to be. I've gotten accustomed to standing on corners & waiting, lying on benches and waiting, standing up in the heart of a forest, or just in the wooded part of a park, and waiting. I've wondered sometimes if you came, and I saw you, and I knew you were there, I'd continue to go on waiting.

It could be like that, but I don't think it would. I don't even think it could be. It couldn't, because if you came, things would change. A thousand, maybe a million things would change. My whole life would change. I know that. I've known that much from the beginning.